Healing Wisdom

50 Prayerful Insights for Living

Pastor & Mrs. Samuel,
Thank you for your ministry.
Happy Reading! Prayerfully
Sim Chor Kiat

by Chor-Kiat Sim, D.Min., B.C.C.
with a preface by Mark Feldbush, M. Div., B.C.C.

Dedication

This book is written in memory of my mentors:
Chester H. Damron, pastor, chaplain, and missionary;
and my granduncle Yeow-Hwee Sim, entrepreneur,
philanthropist, and kinsman who lived an exemplary
life of discipline, integrity and wisdom, demonstrating
the true dedication of the Sim family for relatives and
community.

Xulon Press
2301 Lucien Way #41
Maitland, FL 32751
407.339.4217
www.xulonpress.com

XULON PRESS

Unless otherwise noted, Bible texts are from the New International Version Copyright © 1973, 1978, 1984.

Scripture taken from the New King James Version®.
Copyright © 1982 by Thomas Nelson. Used by permission. All rights reserved.

All other quotations besides the Bible verses are from the writings of Ellen G. White known as the Spirit of Prophecy.

Graphic Design by Rebecca Feldbush, Buckeyegrrl Designs.

All pictures are taken by the author except:
Page 62, Copyright © Dr. Stanley Setiawan.
Cover Photo, Copyright © Straga/Depositphotos.com.

Printed in the United States of America.

ISBN-13: 9781545628249

Introduction

L ife is a journey of both grace and grief. At the moment of our birth into this sinful world, we leave our "comfort zone," our mother's womb. In a sense, grief begins in the very first second of our existence. No one is exempt.

Every second that ticks by brings the unexpected closer. At times, grief engulfs us. Yet other moments bring healing. Through each second, billions of cells work to keep us alive, mending defects and deficits and resisting environmental invasions. Life and death struggles are part of life's journey. Many survive. Others succumb to opposing forces.

Providentially, we have each been ushered into the world with all its sickness and health, losses and deliverance. Life brings awareness that illness is often followed by healing and recovery.

Throughout my life, many Scripture promises have encouraged me and helped bring healing. One of my most cherished verses is found in Isaiah 58:8: "Then your light shall break forth like the dawn, and your healing shall spring up quickly." This promise blesses me with strength, resilience, inspiration, and nurture. It motivates me to seek godliness through prayer. It brought me a sense of hope about fifty years ago, which led to my conversion to Jesus Christ. John 3:16 also became one of my precious promises. You might have treasured and clung to it too.

As we journey through this book, I am honored to have you experience with me the blessings of deliverance from sin and sickness through prayer and Bible study. I pray the content of this book will uplift you as you travel along life's paths of joy and grief. May your life be crowned with health and deliverance.

Let us rejoice as we contemplate these prayers based on Jesus's greatest message: The Sermon on the Mount. Read on and discover the promises of God fulfilled in your life as they have been in mine.

You may ask these questions: **In what way does this text or prayer guide you to know God better? How is this verse or prayer most related to various areas in your life?**

Preface

I have known Dr. Chor-Kiat Sim, a fellow pastor for several years. In 2011, we worked together as staff chaplains at Washington Adventist Hospital in Takoma Park, Maryland. Pastor Sim invited me to review some material that he was working on for a prayer book. His idea was simple enough: a verse of Scripture, an original prayer based on that verse, and a corresponding devotional thought from the writings of Ellen White, a Christian author who considered herself a messenger of the Lord. As I read and edited his prayers, I was struck by the sincerity and honest faith of my friend. His prayers reflected both the majesty and closeness of God.

The result of the Pastor's devotional writing was the book *Purposeful Prayers: Finding Joy in the Journey* that was published in 2012. In the years since then, this beautiful book has been translated into the Chinese and Indonesian languages, and 25,000 copies have been printed. With this book, his other publications on pastoral care and his years pastoring in Singapore and the United States, his ministry has had a global impact.

Pastor Sim continued in his hospital ministry in Maryland and I moved to another hospital in Ohio. Then "life" happened and he found himself confronting some major health concerns. The healer was now in need of healing. Where some would have questioned their faith, he dug deeper into his and it became a sure foundation in the midst of his struggle. As he confronted his humanity, he began writing more prayers. In time, he had enough for a second volume. Pastor Sim once again asked me to review his material. As I read these new prayers, I sensed the strong faith that comes only through struggle. This new book, *Healing Wisdom: 50 Prayerful Insights for Living* offers the reader a chance to encounter God's healing presence in a fresh way. It is my hope that this book will strengthen your faith and service for God, just as it has for my dear friend.

—Mark Feldbush, MDiv, BCC

Disclaimer: The contents in this book are not substitutes for your provider's advice.

Contents

Purposeful Prayers for

Healing &
Deliverance

1. A Prayer for Restoration

Create in me a pure heart, O God,
and renew a steadfast spirit within me. —*Psalm 51:10*

Dear Lord,

Thank You for creating me in Your image. You are an awesome God. Though Your image has been marred in us by sin, You have provided a way of salvation. You restore me with joy through faith. As I continue to travel this journey, may I be able to face the challenges of life. Christ, have mercy on me and forgive my sins so that in Your all-knowing will all my diseases may be healed. You are more than a healer; You are healing. Inspire me to share the good news of Your healing love. In Your holy name, I pray. *Amen.*

Jesus was the spring of my hope and joy and courage. Heaven has seemed to be very near, and Christ the great Physician, my restorer, the remedy of sickness. —*That I May Know Him.* p. 283

Personal Reflections

_____

_____

_____

_____

_____

_____

2. A Prayer for Wholeness

As far as the east is from the west, so far hath He removed our transgressions from us. —*Psalm 103:12*

Dear God, our Father,

I need Your cleansing to restore me to wholeness in You. Sin and its evil forces have fractured me. Destructive forces have horribly impacted me and prevented me from complete restoration. Be very close to me, Almighty God. In Jesus' loving name, I pray. *Amen.*

God in Christ gave Himself for our sins. He suffered the cruel death of the cross, bore for us the burden of guilt, "the just for the unjust," that He might reveal to us His love and draw us to Himself. And He says, "Be ye kind one to another, tenderhearted, forgiving each other, even as God also in Christ forgave you" (Ephesians 4:32, RV).

—*Living in the Sunlight,* p. 59

Personal Reflections

_____

_____

_____

_____

_____

_____

_____

_____

3. A Prayer for Patience

But I tell you, do not swear an oath at all:
either by heaven, for it is God's throne. —*Matthew 5:34*

Dear Lord,

Help me not to use Your name in vain like others who do not know the Creator. Grant me the wisdom to be truthful and grateful to You. There are values You have taught that I cherish: patience, purity, and power from Your unlimited grace. Bless me to be the person You had in mind when You made me. Help me act according to Your will as You did Your Father's will. In Jesus' name, I pray. *Amen.*

Christian lives constantly as in the presence of God, knowing that every thought is open to the eyes of Him with whom we have to do; and when required to do so in a lawful manner, it is right for him to appeal to God as a witness that what he says is the truth, and nothing but the truth. —*Living in the Sunlight,* p. 33

Personal Reflections

4. A Prayer for Spiritual Growth

But I tell you, do not resist an evil person. —*Matthew 5:39*

Compassionate Savior,

You led me to rejoice in You, to repent, to witness for my faith, to share the Gospel, to demonstrate Your character, and to serve fully. Let my prayer be this song: "Spirit of the living God, fall afresh on me, break me, melt me, mold me and fill me. Spirit of the living God, Fall afresh on me."* Indeed, fill me with Your Holy Spirit. That's all I need when adversaries confront me mercilessly. I am forgiving by Your grace. In Jesus' name, I pray. *Amen.*

Those who are imbued with the Spirit of Christ abide in Christ. The blow that is aimed at them falls upon the Savior, who surrounds them with His presence. And from the cross of Calvary there comes down through the ages His prayer for His murderers and the message of hope to the dying thief. —*Living in the Sunlight,* p. 35

Personal Reflections

_____

_____

_____

_____

_____

_____

* Copyright © 1935, 1963 by Moody Press. Moody Bible Institute, Chicago, IL.

5. A Prayer for Generosity

And if anyone wants to sue you and take your shirt,
hand over your coat as well. If anyone forces you to go one mile,
go with him or her two miles. —*Matthew 5:40-41*

Lord of Life,

Grant me the sense of obedience to give generously, especially to those in need. They have their burdens. May I remember to pray for them and be sensitive to their hurts. In Your holy name, I pray. *Amen.*

Jesus bade His disciples, instead of resisting the demands of those in authority, to do even more than was required of them. And, so far as possible, they should discharge every obligation, even if it were beyond what the law of the land required. —*Living in the Sunlight,* p. 36

Personal Reflections

6. A Prayer for Unconditional Love

But I tell you, love your enemies and pray for those who persecute you, that you may be children of your Father in heaven.

—Matthew 5:44

Loving Lord,

Grant me an open heart to embrace those who need Christian maturity. They have their battles to fight. Help me to ask for Your grace and mercy so I can love as You loved the thief on the cross beside You. Grant me an understanding heart. In Jesus' name, I pray. *Amen.*

The children of God are those who are partakers of His nature. It is not earthly rank, nor birth, nor nationality, nor religious privilege, which proves that we are members of the family of God; it is love, a love that embraces all humanity. —*Living in the Sunlight* pp. 37, 38

Personal Reflections

_____

_____

_____

_____

_____

_____

_____

7. A Prayer for Holiness

He causes his sun to rise on the evil and the good,

and sends rain on the righteous and the unrighteous.

—Matthew 5:45

Dear Jesus,

Holy! Holy! Holy! I bow my head and fold my hands, kneeling in adoration. Teach me to be good and to fear no evil, with You beside me. The pain and powerlessness in my challenging illness are ways to shape and transform me so that Your perfection becomes mine. Help me be willing to submit to Your molding. In Your precious name, I pray. *Amen.*

To be kind to the unthankful and to the evil, to do good for nothing again, is the insignia of the royalty of heaven, the sure token by which the children of the Highest reveal their high estate.

—Living the Sunlight, p. 37-38

Personal Reflections

_____

_____

_____

_____

_____

_____

8. A Prayer for Perfection

Be perfect, therefore, as your heavenly Father is perfect.

—*Matthew 5:48*

Dear God Our Father,

You loved me so much that You sent Your Son to die for my sins and save me from destruction. Forgive me of my sins. Grant me an abundant life, so I do not fear disease and pestilence as I know You are by my side. I have no fear of death as You have conquered it. Creator, Jesus Christ, have mercy on me, forgive my sins, and keep me safe. In Your blessed name, I pray. *Amen.*

Thus you will be in harmony with every precept of His law; for "the law of the Lord is perfect, restoring the soul."

—Psalm 19:7, margin

Through love "the righteousness of the law" will be "fulfilled in us, who walk not after the flesh, but after the Spirit" (Romans 8:4).

—*Living the Sunlight*, p. 39

Personal Reflections

_____

_____

_____

_____

_____

Purposeful Prayers for
Deeper
Relationships

1. A Prayer for Authenticity

Be careful not to practice your righteousness in front of others to be seen by them. If you do, you will have no reward from your Father in heaven. —Matthew 6:1

Merciful God, My Father,

How wretched I am, seeking self-glory and praise from others. Transform me by Your grace so that I will serve with authenticity. Teach me to be kind and caring without expecting anything in return. May the Holy Spirit inspire a pure character and true faith. Fill me with Your power and love so that deeds of kindness are done without expecting many rewards. In Jesus' loving name, I pray. *Amen.*

By their good works, Christ's followers are to bring glory, not to themselves, but to Him through whose grace and power they have wrought. It is through the Holy Spirit that every good work is accomplished, and the Spirit is given to glorify, not the receiver, but the Giver. The grace of Christ in the soul is developing traits of character that are the opposite of selfishness, traits that will refine, ennoble, and enrich the life. —*Living in the Sunlight,* p. 41

Personal Reflections

2. A Prayer for Truthfulness

And when you pray, do not be like the hypocrites, for they love to pray standing in the synagogues and on the street corners to be seen by others. Truly I tell you, they have received their reward in full. But when you pray, go into your room, close the door and pray to your Father, who is unseen. Then your Father, who sees what is done in secret, will reward you.

And when you pray, do not keep on babbling like pagans, for they think they will be heard because of their many words.

Do not be like them, for your Father knows what you need before you ask him. —Matthew 6:5-8

Dear Lord,

You are supreme in my life. Motivate me to serve You whole-heartedly. Teach me to pray truthfully and live resiliently. Help me to press forward with "power, love, and discipline" (2 Timothy 1:7). May Your peace and understanding be with me as I move forward in faith. Eternal loving God, fill me with Your love and gratitude. In Jesus' name, I pray. *Amen.*

By maintaining a connection with God, we shall be enabled to diffuse to others, through our association with them, the light, the peace, the serenity, that rule in our hearts. The strength acquired in prayer to God, united with persevering effort in training the mind in thoughtfulness and caretaking, prepares one for daily duties and keeps the spirit in peace under all circumstances.

—*Living in the Sunlight,* p. 43

Personal Reflections

3. A Prayer for Clarity

And when you pray, do not keep on babbling like pagans,
for they think they will be heard because of their many words.

—Matthew 6:7

Dear Lord,

While the repetition of ideas is essential for learning, rote prayers are meaningless. Help me not to repeat prayers without being engaged. May I always be specific in what I request. And Lord, help me not to be jealous of others' achievements. Teach me to love You with all my heart and all my strength. Wisdom that comes from You is more precious than silver or gold. In Your loving name, I pray. *Amen.*

The most eloquent prayers are but idle words if they do not express the true sentiments of the heart. But the prayer that comes from an earnest heart, when the simple wants of the soul are expressed as we would ask an earthly friend for a favor, expecting it to be granted— this is the prayer of faith. *—Living in the Sunlight,* p. 44

Personal Reflections

_____

_____

_____

_____

_____

_____

4. A Prayer for Friendship with God

Do not be like them, for your Father knows what you need before you ask Him.   —*Matthew 6:8*

Dear Jesus Christ, Creator and Redeemer,

Words cannot describe my longing for You. I feel lonely when I am disconnected from You. Such distance disappears when I sense Your presence and seek You with all my heart and find You. Thank You for Your loving, caring, comforting, and gracious presence in moments of despair. In Jesus' loving name, I pray. *Amen.*

God does not desire our ceremonial compliments, but the unspoken cry of the heart broken and subdued with a sense of its sin and utter weakness finds its way to the Father of all mercy.

—*Living in the Sunlight*, p. 44

Personal Reflections

_____

_____

_____

_____

_____

_____

_____

_____

5. A Prayer for Relief

Surely, He has borne our griefs, and carried our sorrows...

—Isaiah 53:4-5

⁓

Eternal Father,

Never before have I so deeply felt the warmth, wisdom, and wonderful assurance of eternal life through the saving grace of Jesus. Thank You, Lord. I am healed and on a journey towards a hope-filled recovery. Help me to follow health principles such as nutrition, exercise, and trust in You as my body is "the temple of the Holy Spirit" (1 Cor. 6:19). Grant me the purity of my body, mind, and spirit. Fill me with the comfort of the Counselor so that I can move forward with confidence and faith to receive the gift of eternal life. In Jesus' name, I pray. *Amen.*

So ready, so eager, is the Savior's heart to welcome us as members of the family of God, that in the very first words we are to use in approaching God He places the assurance of our divine relationship.

—Living in the Sunlight, p. 53

Personal Reflections

Purposeful Prayers
Centered on
Forgiveness

1. A Prayer for Holiness

In this manner, therefore, pray. Our Father in heaven, hallowed be Your name. Your kingdom come. Your will be done, on earth as it is in heaven. Give us today our daily bread. And forgive us our debts, as we also have forgiven our debtors. And do not lead us into temptation, but deliver us from the evil one. For Yours is the kingdom and the power and the glory forever. Amen. —Matthew 6:9-13

Loving Lord Jesus,

You taught us to pray to Your Father. What an honor for me, my family, and my friends to address You personally. Absolve me of my inherited sins. Through Your Father's love, give me a clear conscience so I can commune with You and live a life of purity. I thank You for guidance that enables me to live a holy life, dedicated to serving others. My heart is filled with gratitude as I approach Your throne of grace to find cleansing of my unrighteousness. In Your merciful name, I pray. *Amen.*

We are taught to come to God with our tribute of thanksgiving, to make known our wants, to confess our sins, and to claim His mercy in accordance with His promise. —*Living in the Sunlight*, p. 53

Personal Reflections

2. A Prayer for Providence

Our Father in heaven...   —*Matthew 6:9*

Almighty God the Father,

How honored I am to call You Father. As I experience the vicissitudes of life, going through tests and trials that disrupt my life, You hold me in the hollow of Your hand, which protects and prevents me from worldliness that distracts me from knowing You better. Oh, how I experience such power that strengthens my faith so I can live a righteous and productive life for You. When my life comes to an end, I can say with many of Your believers, I have not lived in vain. In Jesus' holy name, I pray. *Amen.*

We have an Advocate in the heavens, and whoever accepts Him as a personal Saviour is not left an orphan to bear the burden of his own sins. The perception of God's love works the renunciation of selfishness. In calling God our Father, we recognize all His children as our brethren. We are all a part of the great web of humanity, all members of one family.   —*Living in the Sunlight*, p. 53, 54

Personal Reflections

_____

_____

_____

_____

_____

3. A Prayer for Sanctification

Hallowed be Your name...   —*Matthew 6:9*

Holy God and Father,

Your light of righteousness shines brightly from beginning to eternity. I have nothing to fear, except when the world tempts me with worldliness. Keep me pure, knowing what is good and what is evil. Bless me and my family as we endeavor to live a life of purity and integrity. May I constantly look to You for blessings and for sustenance of life. Keep me holy, happy and healthy. In Your wonderful name, I pray. *Amen.*

God has acknowledged you before men and angels as His child; pray that you may do no dishonor to the "worthy name by which ye are called" (James 2:7). God sends you into the world as His representative. In every act of life you are to make manifest the name of God.   —*Living in the Sunlight,* p. 55

Personal Reflections

4. A Prayer for Repentance

Your kingdom come...   *—Matthew 6:10*

Dear Jesus, my Prince of Hope,

My troubled heart yearns for light. Darkness is crowding me with
worries, anxiety, and disappointment. Help me to focus on the beauty
of Your creation, like each morning's sunrise, a daily demonstration of
hope. I look forward to the day when sun, moon, and stars will shine
without being obscured and my heart will no longer be shrouded
in darkness. Help me to follow Your way of life and to reflect with
understanding. Transform me through repentance. Help me to find
safety under Your wings. You have paid a price so that we can find
hope in hopelessness. None of this is possible without Your shed blood
cleansing me from sin. I look forward with joy to the blessed hope
of Your Second Coming. In Your precious name, I pray. *Amen.*

**The heavenly gates are again to be lifted up, and with ten thousand
times ten thousand and thousands of thousands of holy ones, our
Saviour will come forth as King of kings and Lord of lords. Jehovah
Immanuel "shall be king over all the earth" (Zechariah 14: 9).**

—Living in the Sunlight, p. 56

Personal Reflections

5. A Prayer for Salvation

Your will be done on earth as it is in heaven...   —*Matthew 6:10*

Dear God the Father,

Thank You for Your promises that bring comfort to my troubled heart. I will pray without ceasing for Your will be done, to fulfill Your righteous promise for me. Divine Lord, have mercy on me if I have taken Your power for granted. Your promise to bring blessings on earth as in heaven is amazing. Forgive me for doubting all that You can do through me. Almighty God the Father, You are everything to me and my life is in Your hands forever. In Christ's saving grace, I pray. *Amen.*

Jesus bade His disciples, instead of resisting the demands of those in authority, to do even more than was required of them. And, so far as possible, they should discharge every obligation, even if it were beyond what the law of the land required.

—*Living in the Sunlight*, p. 36

Personal Reflections

---

6. A Prayer for Provisions

Give us this today our daily bread. —*Matthew 6:11*

Dear Jesus, my Lord,

You are the Bread of Life that nourishes my body, mind, and spirit. You created me to be in constant need of filling my thirst for the freshness of love. You satisfy my hunger for relationships, for meaning, for strength, for faith and for hope. It is only through You that I can receive the joys and spiritual fruit You promised.

Continue to shower me with the peace You promised. Help me to be mindful of my sins and wrong choices that prevent me from receiving You, the eternal Bread and the living Water that I long for. May Your name be glorified as I fill myself with heavenly provisions. In Your precious name, I pray. *Amen.*

If you have renounced self and given yourself to Christ you are a member of the family of God, and everything in the Father's house is for you. All the treasures of God are opened to you, both the world that now is and that which is to come. The ministry of angels, the gift of His Spirit, the labors of His servants—all are for you. The world, with everything in it, is yours so far as it can do you good. Even the enmity of the wicked will prove a blessing by disciplining you for heaven. If "ye are Christ's... all things are yours." (1 Corinthians 3:23, 21).   —*Living the Sunlight,* p. 57

Personal Reflections

7. A Prayer for Forgiveness

Forgive us our debts, as we also have forgiven our debtors.

—Matthew 6:12

Lord Emmanuel,

Be with me today, another day when many are suffering, traumatized, abused, intimidated, scared or even killed for living an innocent life. I am grateful to You, my King of kings, who saves me and restores me from sickness and sin. Heal me from physical and emotional wounds caused by friends or foes alike through Your forgiveness. Grant me a portion of Your grace to empathize with those who wrong me. Teach me to open my arms of forgiveness so that our estrangement can be turned to harmony. Thus, life can be more livable and joys can be more attainable. You have marvelously and wonderfully made me (Psalm 136:14). In Your awesome name, I pray. *Amen.*

Forgiveness, reconciliation with God, comes to us, not as a reward for our works, it is not bestowed because of the merit of sinful men, but it is a gift unto us, having in the spotless righteousness of Christ its foundation for bestowal....We should not try to lessen our guilt by excusing sin. We must accept God's estimate of sin, and that is heavy indeed. Calvary alone can reveal the terrible enormity of sin. If we had to bear our own guilt, it would crush us. But the sinless One has taken our place; though undeserving, He has borne our iniquity. "If we confess our sins, [God] is faithful and just to forgive us our sins, and to cleanse us from all unrighteousness" (1 John 1:9).

—*Living the Sunlight*, p. 60

Personal Reflections

8. A Prayer for Victory

And lead us not into temptation... —*Matthew 6:13*

❧

Son of God,

In times of uncertainties, grant me an anchor in You so that I can be decisive and move forward with faith, hope, and love. Grant me also courage to face crises in life. I need to be strong and face the future with greater boldness. Having You as a constant companion on my life journey is what I need. With Your help, I will not allow distractions of any kind to linger. Shield me from temptations. I am in Your care and keeping; help me be calm, relaxed, and restful, including on the Sabbath. You have enriched my life and met my needs. In You, I have victory and reasons to rejoice over Your blessings in my life. Loving Creator, Jesus Christ, have mercy on me. In Your precious name, I pray. *Amen.*

Thank God, we are not left alone. He who "so loved the world, that He gave His only-begotten Son, that whosoever believeth in Him should not perish, but have everlasting life" (John 3:16), will not desert us in the battle with the adversary of God. —*Living in the Sunlight,* p. 62

Personal Reflections

---

9. A Prayer for Deliverance

But deliver us from the evil one. —*Matthew 6:13*

Eternal God the Father,

You invite me to face the future positively. I trust You for deliverance. Moreover, I consider it pure joy because the testing of my faith produces perseverance. Such challenges will make me mature, complete, and blessed (James 1:2-4, 12). I love You, Lord, and claim the promise of forgiveness. Help me to have a clear mind while journeying with You. Compassionate God, may I be aware of Your delivering me from darkness. Grant me Your heavenly peace (John 14:27). Help me to praise You with songs of deliverance such as those found in the Psalms. May the Holy Spirit abide in me always. In the wonderful name of Jesus I pray. *Amen.*

Behold, He says, "I give unto you power to tread on serpents and scorpions, and over all the power of the enemy: and nothing shall by any means hurt you." (Luke 10:19). Live in contact with the living Christ, and He will hold you firmly by a hand that will never let go.
—*Living in the Sunlight*, p. 62

Personal Reflections

_____

_____

_____

_____

10. A Prayer for Glory

Yours is the kingdom and the power and the glory forever.

—Matthew 6:13 NKJV

$\backsim$

Dear Christ Jesus,

You are my Creator and Redeemer. I come to You again with pain in my heart, feeling overwhelmed by manipulation and accusations. Nevertheless, Your love prevails. By Your grace, I find dignity in the midst of opposition. Lord and Saviour, it is through You that I find continuous growth, faith, and joy. It is through Your Spirit that I experience transformation. Jesus, come into my ailing heart. Cleanse me by Your grace with the light of the Cross so that I may be able to live forever. In Your glorious name, I pray. *Amen.*

He will thwart the purposes of wicked men, and will bring to confusion the counsels of those who plot mischief against His people. He who is the King, the Lord of hosts, sitteth between the cherubim, and amid the strife and tumult of nations He guards His children still. He is our Savior, and His people will be safe in His hands.

—Living in the Sunlight, p. 63

Personal Reflections

_____

_____

_____

_____

Purposeful Prayers for
Confidence

1. A Prayer for Understanding

For if you forgive other people when they sin against you, your heavenly Father will also forgive you. But if you do not forgive others their sins, your Father will not forgive your sins. —Matthew 6:14-15

Dear Lord,

The prayer You taught Your disciples inspires me with understanding. It reveals Your identity, authority, forgiveness, and victory. Forgive my resistance at times to Your leading. Show me Your greatness. By Your grace, grant me the ability to leave troubles in the past and to see the value of genuine relationships. With humility, may I make things right. As I move forward in sanctification along my Christian journey, to You be the glory. In Your blessed name, I pray. *Amen.*

It is "God's forgiveness that first made it possible for me" to restore fractured relationships. "The discovery of [God's] forgiveness released me from the emotional turmoil that would otherwise have consumed me." —Lourdes E. Morales, *Gudmundsson, I forgive you, but...*, p. 17

Personal Reflections

_____

_____

_____

_____

_____

_____

_____

2. A Prayer for Trust

Therefore, I tell you, do not worry about your life, what you will eat or drink; or about your body, what you will wear. Is not life more than food, and the body more than clothes? Look at the birds of the air; they do not sow or reap or store away in barns, and yet your heavenly Father feeds them. Are you not much more valuable than they? Can any one of you by worrying add a single hour to your life?

—Matthew 6:25-27

Eternal God, my Father,

I am Your servant, completely committed to You as Your son. As such I am Your steward, Your witness, and Your instrument of peace. Grant me Your peace that surpasses all understanding (Phil. 4:7) and love that conquers fear (1 John 4:18). May I be a channel of hope. Help me to share the gift of the Good News of eternal life from Jesus. Living fully for You inspires me to live for Your glory and honor. In Your Son's precious name, I pray. *Amen.*

Yet Christ's followers were not to fear that their hope was lost or that God had forsaken the earth. The disciples of Christ were directed to look above all the power and dominion of evil to the Lord their God, whose kingdom rules overall and who is their Father and everlasting Friend. —*Living in the Sunlight*, p. 62

Personal Reflections

3. A Prayer for Faith

Therefore, do not worry about tomorrow, for tomorrow will worry about itself. Each day has enough trouble of its own.

—*Matthew 6:34*

O God, My Heavenly Father,

How often I worry about many things, including that my voice has not been heard. It is hearing Your voice that keeps me calm. Therefore, listening more than speaking keeps me out of trouble. When Your voice of faith, love, and hope is heard, Your peace fills my heart. Teach me to live one day at a time in Your abundant grace. May Your glory be magnified now and till eternity. In Christ's name, I pray. *Amen.*

He will thwart the purposes of wicked human beings and will bring to confusion the counsels of those who plot mischief against His people. He who is the king, the Lord of host, will amid the strife and tumult of nations guard His children still. He is our Savior, and His people will be safe in His hands. —*Living in the Sunlight,* p. 63

Personal Reflections

_____

_____

_____

_____

_____

_____

4. A Prayer for Optimisim

Do not judge, or you too will be judged. For in the same way you judge others, you will be judged, and with the measure you use, it will be measured to you. —*Matthew 7:1*

Forgiving God, My Father,

I pray that You renew my mind in Christ Jesus (Rom. 12:2). May my every thought, word, or action reveal the greatest miracle in the cleansing power of the Spirit in my heart. Help me to be concerned with my responsibilities and not to place blame on others. For blaming is blind! May Your forgiveness purify me from sinful indulgences. It is Your grace that radiates from the Cross of Calvary that makes a brighter future possible. In Jesus' name, I pray. *Amen.*

We cannot read the heart. Ourselves faulty, we are not qualified to sit in judgment upon others. Finite human beings can judge only from outward appearance. To him alone who knows the secret springs of action, and who deals tenderly and compassionately, is it given to decide the case of every soul. —*Living in the Sunlight,* p. 64

Personal Reflections

_____

_____

_____

_____

_____

5. A Prayer for Insights

Why do you look at the speck of sawdust in your brother's eye
and pay no attention to the plank in your own eye? —*Matthew 7:3*

Dear Jesus,

You are the only true standard of character. Keep me humble so that
I may see Your light that shines in darkness—light that illuminates my
path. This is the light that builds the bridge between You and humanity.
As I learn more about reflection and faith development, teach me to
embrace resilience. Help me to have enduring love that I may devote
myself fully in Your service in response to Your redeeming loves. Your
sacrificing love on the Cross of Calvary inspires me to be faithful.
The only way I am able to live with a forgiving spirit is by Your never-
ending grace. May Your healing wisdom be glorious in the sunshine
of Your love. Lord, I surrender all to You. In Your holy name, I pray.
Amen.

**Christ is the only true standard of character. Finding itself destitute of
the power of love, it has reached out for the strong arm of the state to
enforce its dogmas and execute its decrees.**

—*Living in the Sunlight*, p. 65

Personal Reflections

_____

_____

_____

_____

6. A Prayer for Focus

Do not give dogs what is sacred; do not throw your pearls to pigs. If you do, they may trample them under their feet, and then turn and tear you in pieces. —Matthew 7:6

Dear Lord,

Quiet my sometimes wild thoughts. Heal me from the negative impacts of the traumatic events I experienced in my past. Show me the Way, the Truth, and the Life (John 14:6). This will enable me to seek to be in Your kingdom by Your righteousness. Teach me to remember the lessons of faith in the school of Christ. Let the Gospel bring me transformation. And may I learn from You that no matter how misled I am, You can rescue me from the peril of sin. In this way, I can focus my attention on You. In Your gracious name, I pray. *Amen.*

Every promise in the Word of God furnishes us with subject matter for prayer, presenting the pledged word of Jehovah as our assurance. Whatever Spiritual blessing we need, it is our privilege to claim through Jesus. We may tell the Lord, with the simplicity of a child, exactly what we need. —*Living in the Sunlight*, p. 69

Personal Reflections

_____

_____

_____

_____

7. A Prayer for Refinement

Ask, and it will be given to you; seek and you will find;
knock and the door will be opened to you. —*Matthew 7:7*

Eternal God, My Father,

Bless me with a stronger desire to "be like Jesus" — to be like Your Son whose character is matchless and flawless. Perfect! Purify my thoughts and refine me. Teach me righteousness by Your divine example. May the hymn "Live out Thy Life within Me"* be the theme of my life. May I be empowered by You to seek Your love and refinement. With this direction, may I overcome selfishness and passivity when action is needed. May I find direction in the wilderness of harsh human circumstances. Fill me with spiritual strength, heavenly vision and uplifting thoughts. Lord, guide my every step. Enable me to be honest and virtuous in Christ with prayerful insights for living. May I live with integrity. Fill me with rich wisdom and discipline. To You be the glory, O God, in Christ's name I pray. *Amen.*

Your heavenly Father knows that you have need of all things, and you are invited to ask Him concerning them. It is through the name of Jesus that every favor is received. God will honor that name and will supply your necessities from the riches of His liberality.

—*Living in the Sunlight,* p. 69

Personal Reflections

_____

_____

* Frances Ridley Havergal, *SDA Hymnal*, p. 316.

8. A Prayer for Change

So in everything, do to others what you would have them do to you,
for this sums up the Law and the Prophets. —*Matthew 7:12*

Dear Creator Jesus Christ:

As I acknowledge my fear of death and dying, grief overwhelms me.
There were also thoughts of loss and respect. Lord Jesus, I trust
in You and have faith in You as You as the owner of the universe. I pray
that You calm my spirit so that, instead of living in fear, I count my
blessings. Help me to refuse unbelief and let You reign over me. Lord,
thank You for Your blessed gift of transformation and sustenance for
me. Help me to focus on how You have nurtured me through Your
Holy Word and the Spirit of Prophecy. In Jesus' loving name, I pray.
Amen.

**In your association with others, put yourself in their place. Enter into
their feelings, their difficulties, their disappointments, their joys, and
their sorrows. Identify yourself with them, and then do to them as
you would wish them to deal with you.** —*Living in the Sunlight,* p. 70

Personal Reflections

9. A Prayer for Direction

But small is the gate and narrow the road that leads to life,
and only a few find it. —*Matthew 7:14*

Eternal Lord Jesus,

Help me to be what You want me to be and follow Your direction. I remember You turned water to refreshing wine. Similarly, tranforming my waywardness into Christ's mission of seeking and saving. Help me not to seek self-gratification or be jealous of others' success. I ask daily that the peace You give me will bring healing. Guide me in mapping a path of healing towards recovery.

May I pray daily for self-understanding and conversion: no envy, greed, or covetousness as part of my life. Teach me to live with wisdom and power. May I cherish the love of my family. Restore the damage done by others who attempted to jeopardize my plans. Help me regain my sense of direction by trusting in your power. Let the love of Jesus fill me and allow me in return to bless others. In Your loving name, I pray. *Amen*

In the road to death the whole race may go, with all their worldliness, selfishness, pride, dishonesty, and moral abasement. There is room for everyone's opinions, and doctrines, space to follow one's own inclinations, to do whatever self-love may dictate. As for the path that leads to destruction, there is no need to search for it. Its gate is wide, and the way is broad, and the feet naturally turn into the path that ends in death. —*Living in the Sunlight*, p. 72

Personal Reflections

10. A Prayer for Foundation

The rain came down, the streams rose, and the winds blew and beat against that house; yet it did not fall, because it had its foundation on the rock.   —*Matthew 7:25*

My Lord and my God,

How great You are! I am confessing my sins and feeling the poverty of my soul. May You awaken in me a clearer understanding of Your truth, allowing You to make our relationship even more meaningful. I need help to witness for You in a timely and genuine manner. May Your Word and wisdom be part of my life because You are my solid foundation. Bless my family and me, O Lord. In Jesus' name, I pray. *Amen.*

Like the builders of those houses on the rock, said Jesus, are those who shall receive the words that I have spoken to you, and make them the foundation of their character and life. Centuries before, the prophet Isaiah had written. "The word of God stands forever" **(Isaiah 40:8).**   —*Living in the Sunlight,* p. 78

Personal Reflections

11. A Prayer for the Living Word

Therefore, everyone who hears these words of mine and puts them into practice is like a wise man who built his house on the rock.

—*Matthew 7:24*

Almighty God the Father,

Help me to be inspired by the power of the Living Word. Like the sun and the moon submit to the order of the King of the universe, Your words have shone and impact the human race from the beginning of time. Your words that affect life like the moon affects the ebb and flow of tides and the sun that provides life to all living things. Lord, God the Father, let the whole earth value Your holy Word. It communicates Your leading, caring, and power now and forever. In Jesus, our Creator and Redeemer's name, I pray. *Amen.*

Christ, the true foundation, is a living stone. His life is imparted to all that are built upon Him. "You also, as living stones, are being built up a spiritual house" (1 Peter 2:5). "The whole building, being fitted together, grows into a holy temple in the Lord" (Ephesians 2:21). The stones became one with the foundation.

—*Living in the Sunlight,* p. 79

Personal Reflections

12. A Prayer for Intelligence

Then I will tell them plainly, "I never knew you. Away from me,
you evildoers!" —*Matthew 7:23*

Loving Redeemer, My Lord Jesus,

Thank You for Your love, Jesus my Lord; You are the spring of joy,
hope, and courage. Help me not to fret over those who prosper or
succeed. Help me claim my own authority, enriched by Your power.
Thank You for my wonderful family, caring relatives and friends. Keep
me humble and contrite, recognizing You as my vine and I am Your
branch. May I overcome any tendency to be judgmental. You are
the only judge who knows the secrets of every human heart. Loving
Jesus, bless my family and me. Also may I be more perseverant and
patient with hope of healing and whole recovery through You. In Your
gracious name, I pray. *Amen.*

Those who build on the foundation of human ideas and opinions,
of forms and human ceremonies, or on any works independent of
the grace of Christ are erecting the structure of character upon
shifting sand. —*Living in the Sunlight*, p. 79

Personal Reflections

Purposeful Prayers for

Healing Miracles

1. A Prayer for Obedience

Then Jesus said to him, "See that you don't tell anyone.
But go, show yourself to the priest and offer the gift
Moses commanded, as a testimony to them." —*Matthew 8:4*

Dear Lord,

Help me to be more obedient to Your Word. Reflectively, I realize
I fight hard to win others' approval instead of just being concerned
with Your favor. Lord, take away my pride and selfishness. Grant me
the grace to know the truth of the Gospel that sets me free (John
8:32). Help me to learn more about Your grace, and obey You daily.
In Your holy name, I pray. *Amen.*

**Looking upon the cross, at the humiliations and sufferings endured
in bearing our sins, that His righteousness might be imputed to us,
soften the heart and fill the soul with His love....**
                              —*That I May Know Him,* p. 283

Personal Reflections

_____

_____

_____

_____

_____

_____

2. A Prayer for Confidence

When Jesus came into Peter's house, he saw Peter's mother-in-law lying in bed with a fever. —Matthew 8:14

Dear Healer, My Lord,

I ask You for confidence and wisdom, realizing that my true repentance and daily conversion are essential. Grant me wisdom in the battle of life. Jesus Christ, always be by my side in crisis. May I move forward with Your blessed assurance so as to attain calmness, faith, hope, and joy. In Your loving name, I pray. *Amen.*

I have had during my sleepless hours the most precious contemplations of the love of God to man, expressed in the wonderful sacrifice made to save him from ruin. I love to repeat the name of Jesus; how full of sweetness light, and love it is!
—*That I May Know Him,* p. 283

Personal Reflections

_____

_____

_____

_____

_____

_____

_____

3. A Prayer for Longsuffering

That it might be fulfilled which was spoken by Isaiah the prophet, saying "He Himself took our infirmities and bore our sicknesses."

—Matthew 8:17

My God of Miraculous Healing,

I believe that I am whole in Jesus, free from sin and sickness. Help me not to harbor any doubts that hinder me from restoration. Fill me with the Holy Spirit so that Your spiritual fruits, including longsuffering, will be manifested (Galatians 5:22-23). May the hurts that have wounded me be doors of opportunity to heal my afflictions because You have taken my infirmities. Cleanse me of my sins. Grant me the courage to face challenges. Inspire me to see light beyond darkness and to experience Your miracle of healing. In Your wonderful name, I pray. *Amen.*

When pain has seemed to be almost unbearable, I have looked to Jesus and prayed most earnestly, and He has been beside me, and the darkness has passed away and all has seemed the light.
—That I May Know Him, p. 283

Personal Reflections

_____

_____

_____

_____

4. A Prayer for Persistence

"Pick up your stretcher and go home, for you are healed."

—*Matthew 9:6*

My Eternal God and Healer,

Out of my pain, I call upon You, and I sense Your presence. I also experience relief from guilt as You have forgiven me. What a great physician You are to transform my doubt to faith, my hopelessness to hope, and my disappointment to the gift of love. By appreciating Your persistent faith, I feel Your arms of compassion holding me in my distress and abandonment. Restore my health and heal my wounds. (Jeremiah 30:10-20). In Jesus' precious name, I pray. *Amen.*

Jesus is the spring of my hope and my joy and courage. Heaven has seemed to be very near, and Christ the great Physician, my restorer, the remedy of all sickness. In Him all fullness dwells.

—*That I May Know Him,* p. 283

Personal Reflections

_____

_____

_____

_____

_____

_____

_____

5. A Prayer for Renewal

A new heart also will I give you,
and a new spirit will I put within you. —*Ezekiel 36:26*

Dear Gracious God,

Empower me with the courage to see my wretchedness. Cast away my sins that I will be a new creation in Christ (2 Corinthians 5:17). Fill me with the fullness of Your Spirit. Through Your spiritual lens, my eyes are opened to see a heavenly vision: the stars of enlightenment and rainbows of hope. May the bright colors of love, joy, peace, longsuffering, kindness, goodness, faithfulness, gentleness, and self-control renew me (Galatians 5:22-23). Gracious Jesus, thank You for enabling me to live and walk with Your Holy Spirit. *Amen.*

"Though your sins be as scarlet, they shall be as white as snow; though they be red light crimson, they shall be as wool." —Isaiah 1:18

You have confessed your sins, and in heart put them away. you have resolved to give yourself to God. Now go to Him, and ask that He will wash away your sins and give you a new heart. —*Steps to Christ,* p. 32

Personal Reflections

Purposeful Prayers of

Faith &

Resilience

1. A Prayer for Humility

Blessed are the poor in spirit, for theirs is the kingdom of heaven.

—Matthew 5:3

Jesus Christ, My Lord,

I come to You, feeling helpless and hopeless. In humility and trust, I ask that You help me understand any pride in me that needs to be removed. Connect my mind with Your infinite one which governs everything in creation by Your will and word. I claim this promise, "For thus saith the high and lofty One, that inhabiteth eternity, Your name is Holy; I dwell in the high and holy place, with him also that is of a contrite and humble spirit, to revive the spirit of the humble, and to revive the heart of the contrite ones" (Isaiah 57:15). In Your most mighty name, I pray. *Amen.*

One fountain only has been opened for sin, a fountain for the poor in spirit. The proud heart strives to earn salvation; but both our title to heaven and our fitness for it are found in the righteousness of Christ. The Lord can do nothing toward the recovery of man until, convinced of his own weakness, and stripped of all self-sufficiency, he yields himself to the control of God. —*Desire of Ages,* p. 274-275

Personal Reflections

_____

_____

_____

_____

2. A Prayer for Comfort

Blessed are they that mourn: for they shall be comforted.

—Matthew 5:4

Heavenly Father,

Continue to heal my grief through Your Son, the Healer, who provides my healing. Help me to see that You have grieved over the fallen creation and the corruption of humankind. Through the forgiving and redeeming power of Christ, You fill me with comfort and spiritual insights to lean on. Your assurance has transformed my doubts and fears to faith and hope. May the experience of growth through mourning for my sins be a source of renewal. In Jesus' healing name, I pray. *Amen.*

While we sorrow on account of sin, we are to rejoice in the precious privilege of being children of God. And for those also who mourn in trial and sorrow there is comfort. The bitterness of grief and humiliation is better than the indulgences of sin. Through affliction God reveals to us the plague spots in our characters, that by His grace we may overcome our faults. —*Desire of Ages,* p. 275

Personal Reflections

---

3. A Prayer for Meekness

Blessed are the meek, for they shall inherit the earth.

—*Matthew 5:5*

Merciful Lord,

I pray that through Your greatness, You will make known to me the meekness and virtues that connect me with You. Help me to accept Your reproof and heed Your counsels. You have invited me to come to You. In Your gentle spirit, I can find Your rest, comfort and warmth. In Your precious name, I pray. *Amen.*

Lowliness of heart is the strength that gives victory to the followers of Christ; it is the token of their connection with the courts above. "Though the Lord be high, yet hath He respect unto the lowly." (Psalms 138:6). Those who reveal the meek and lowly spirit of Christ are tenderly regarded by God. —*Desire of Ages,* p. 277

Personal Reflections

----

4. A Prayer for Righteousness

Blessed are they which do hunger and thirst after righteousness, for they shall be filled. —Matthew 5:6

⁓

Loving Jesus,

Grant me a sense of unworthiness that will inspire my heart to hunger and thirst for Your righteousness. Then this desire will not be disappointed. Make more room in my heart for You. Then I will realize Your love. I long to bear the likeness of Your character. May the Holy Spirit never leave me, dear Jesus. Help me to understand the things of eternal value and keep my eyes fixed on You, through the work of the Spirit. In Your awesome name, I pray. *Amen.*

If the eye is kept fixed on Christ, the work of the Spirit ceases not until the soul is confounded to His image. The pure element of love will not rest short of the fullness. —*Desire of Ages,* p. 277

Personal Reflections

_____

_____

_____

_____

_____

_____

_____

5. A Prayer for Mercy

Blessed are the merciful, for they shall obtain mercy.   —*Matthew 5:7*

Merciful God,

May my focus on You never cease until my soul is conformed
to Your image. As the pure element of love expands my soul, give
me a capacity for higher attainments. I ask for increased knowledge
of heavenly things, so that my experience may realize Your fullness.
In Your gracious name, I pray. *Amen.*

**The merciful shall find mercy, and the pure in heart shall see God.
Every impure thought defiles the soul, impairs the moral sense, and
tends to obliterate the impressions of the Holy Spirit. All impurity
of speech or thought must be shunned by him who would have clear
discernment of spiritual truth.**   —*Desire of Ages,* p. 278

Personal Reflections

6. A Prayer for Purity

Blessed are the pure in heart, for they shall see God.   —*Matthew 5:8*

⌒

My Creator,

I am grateful for Your grace in which there is forgivenes, and
encouragement. Your presence and listening ear strengthens me.
You rescue me when I fail. Your holiness and loving friendship inspire
joy in my heart. Your way is the only way to purity and eternity. Lord,
keep me safe in the hollow of Your hands. In Jesus' holy name, I pray.
Amen.

**The Lord may and does forgive the repenting sinner; but though
forgiven, the soul is marred. All impurity of speech or of thought
must be shunned by him who would have clear discernment of
spiritual truth.**   —*Desire of Ages,* p. 278

Personal Reflections

_____

_____

_____

_____

_____

_____

_____

_____

_____

7. A Prayer for Peace

Blessed are the peacemakers,
for they shall be called the sons of God.   —*Matthew 5:9*

Christ, my Lord,

Grant me peace that I may know You as the Way, the Truth, and the
Life. It is through harmony with You that I can find peace in my heart.
Lord, "the world is at enmity with the law of God; sinners are at
enmity with their Maker; and as a result they are at enmity with one
another."* Grant me great peace by Your grace from Calvary's cross,
and in obedience to Your law, may no trace of guilt be found in me.
In Your wonderful name I pray. *Amen.*

**Men cannot manufacture peace. Human plans for the purification
and uplifting of individuals or of society will fail of producing peace,
because they do not reach the heart. The only power that can create
or perpetuate true peace is the grace of Christ.**   —*Desire of Ages,* p. 278

Personal Reflections

_____

_____

_____

_____

_____

_____

* *Desire of Ages,* p. 302

8. A Prayer for Resilience

Blessed are they which are persecuted for righteousness' sake: for theirs is the kingdom of heaven. Blessed are ye, when men shall revile you, and persecute you, and shall say all manner of evil against you falsely, for My sake. —*Matthew 5:10-11*

❧

Dear Jesus Christ, My Lord,

The world is sinful and full of hostility to You, Lord. All who worship You will be persecuted, but Your presence is constant. In my darkest hours of peril, You are with me. Your way of mercy and grace lead me to glory. I can face all disturbing elements and oppositions in my fellowship with You. May Your light sweep away the darkness of sin and bring transformation by the influence of the Holy Spirit. As my war against sin leads me to victory, let my faith stand as a witness to others. In Your blessed name, I pray. *Amen.*

Each fiery trial is God's agent for their refining. Each is fitting them for their work as co-laborers with Him. —*Desire of Ages,* p. 279

Personal Reflections

9. A Prayer for Courage

Rejoice, and be exceeding glad: for great is your reward in heaven:
for so persecuted they the prophets which were before you."

—*Matthew 5:12*

෴

Almighty God,

No strife and accusation will discourage me, because I know that
You are the Victor. I experience fellowship with You now, bearing the
reproach of righteousness and attempting the path that You and the
prophets walked while on earth. In sorrow and difficulty, I can rejoice
because You walked the way before me. In Your gracious name, I pray.
Amen.

**Each conflict has its place in the great battle for righteousness, and
each will add to the joy of their final triumph.**   —*Desire of Ages*, p. 279

Personal Reflections

10. A Prayer for Steadfastness

Therefore everyone who hears these words of mine and puts them into practice is like a wise man who built his house on the rock. The rain came down, the streams rose, and the winds blew and beat against that house; yet it did not fall, because it had its foundation on the rock. —*Matthew 7:24-25*

Eternal God, Savior and Redeemer,

You have chosen me and I have responded to rest in Your care. Through nature, You show me Your protection for birds, flowers and all creatures on earth. You are the great Master Artist that displayed the beauty and glory, dear Jesus. I desire to learn more of Your character and long to see my children reveal a character after Your similitude. I pray that all in my family choose Your kingdom of love, righteousness and peace, making You above all other things. May all our motivation be of eternal values, and may every blessing needed for this life be realized through Your providence. I cherish the reality that they are in Your heart and mind. Therefore, with absolute faith, without anxiety or fear, I entrust them to You (Matthew 6:34). May my family and I follow You day by day. In the name of Jesus Christ, my Creator, my Rock and my Redeemer, I pray. *Amen.*

Thus Christ set forth the principles of His kingdom, and showed them to be the great rule of life. To impress the lesson He adds an illustration. It is not enough, He says, for you to hear My words. By obedience you must make them the foundation of your character. Self is but shifting sand.... Receive Me; build on My words.

—*Desire of Ages*, p. 289-290

Personal Reflections

Epilogue

"In His Sermon on the Mount, Christ taught His disciples precious lessons in regard to the necessity of trusting in God. Referring to the works of Christ, John the evangelist wrote, "These are written, that ye might believe that Jesus is the Christ, the Son of God; and that believing ye might have life through His name" (John 20:31). Quoted below is one of many biblical accounts: the story of the paralytic at Bethesda who was paralyzed for thirty-eight years. Yet Jesus bade him, "Rise, take up your bed, and walk" (John 5:8).

"He willed to walk, and he did walk. He acted on the word of Christ." * The man with paralysis believed Christ's word without hesitation. By his faith, Jesus had made him whole at once. It was God's power. It was God who made him whole.

May Jesus, the Author of our being, the Preserver of our life who spoke the Sermon on the Mount, bless the prayers of every reader so they may experience restoration and wholeness.

As you read the *Healing Wisdom: 50 Prayerful Insights for Living*, the gifts of heaven are bestowed to you. Blessings are awaiting your claim and acceptance of Christ and His promises. Christ desires to commune with us with unlimited love. Christ said, "Behold, I stand at the door, and knock: if anyone hears My voice, and opens the door, I will come in and dine with him, and he with Me" (Revelation 3:20 NJKV).

For you who are resting your hope on the promises of Christ and are centered on His words, God's saving grace never fails. The Lord assures us with His forgiveness of all our sins and healing power over all our diseases. (Psalms 103:1-3). May you be blessed as you read and reflect on each Bible text, quotation, and prayer.

It is my hope that this book will enhance your life and cause you to live for Christ more purposefully. In your daily communion with God, listen to His voice. Embrace faith, hope, and love as your most cherished virtues. I pray for you to have a closer walk with Christ and live according to the holy Bible that is the lamp unto your feet and the light unto your path (Psalms 119:10).

*Steps to Christ, pp. 51, 123-124

Acknowledgements

This book is the fruit of many people's encouragement. I continue to appreciate the prayerful life and dedication of Winnie, my wife of forty-five Years, whom I appreciate more and more each new day. The gifts of Gillian, Ginny, and Genny, our three lovely married daughters, and their husbands, have never ceased to be a source of wisdom and patience. Our four granddaughters and two grandsons fill me with joy through the simple fact of their being. Above all, I thank God because through Him I find life meaningful. He helps me to endure hardship and sickness which tax my ability to cope. It is by God's grace that I am still alive.

I am grateful to Jean Ibanez and Mark Feldbush, my former colleagues in chaplaincy ministries. Without their prayerful and editorial support, I would not have written this book. I appreciate Ann Roda, Vice-President and Vladimir Corea, Spiritual Care Director, for their spiritual leadership at Adventist HealthCare. They have led many staff within our healthcare system to have a renewed sense of the mission of Christ. Their leadership provided me opportunities to write prayers and contribute to the spiritual and professional growth of our colleagues in ministry.

There are many colleagues and chaplain interns whom I supervised that inspired me to expand my vision for the Lord's service. God has providentially led Lori Engel, chaplain, and June Carnegie, copy editor, who blessed me with editorial support and patience to publish this book. Dr. Washington Johnson II, Assistant Director, Adventist Chaplaincy Ministries of North America Division, who encouraged me to write this book. He described my book as *"inspiring and a timeless 'a must read' for everyone."* Katherine Walton, Prayer Advocate, has also affirmed me: *"God is using you in such a mighty way to share His grace."*

Prayerfully, it is my hope that because of this book, readers will embrace prayer and Bible study as daily essentials for success. There are many others whose exemplary lives never cease to motivate me to live a purposeful life for our Lord and Savior Jesus Christ.

—C.K. Sim

About the Author

Chor-Kiat "C.K." Sim, D. Min. served as a Seventh-day Adventist church pastor and leader in Singapore before he immigrated to the United States. Prior to his call to be a chaplain at Washington Adventist Hospital in May 1998, he was trained in Clinical Pastoral Education (CPE) at the Cleveland Clinic, Cleveland, Ohio, which prepared him to be a chaplain and CPE supervisor.

For twenty years, Dr. Sim served as a staff chaplain and CPE educator— primarily at Washington Adventist Hospital–Adventist HealthCare. He has touched many lives while fulfilling his calling. Through his rich experience, he published many articles for professional magazines and a book entitled: *Purposeful Prayers: Finding Joy in the Journey* (2012). He and his wife, Winnie, have three married daughters and six grandchildren. The goal of his ministry is to link paths and fulfill dreams for those who desire to learn.

Dr. Sim was recognized by the Association of Professional Chaplains for his "outstanding contributions, leadership and professional service" in February 2009. In November 2016, he received the "Extraordinary Clinical Leadership Ministry Award" from the senior leadership of Adventist HealthCare. To his surprise, he received the "Unsung Hero" Award in September 2017 from the Washington Metro Area Women's Ministries Committee as one of the "Men of Honor" in the community. He felt very honored to have received these awards.

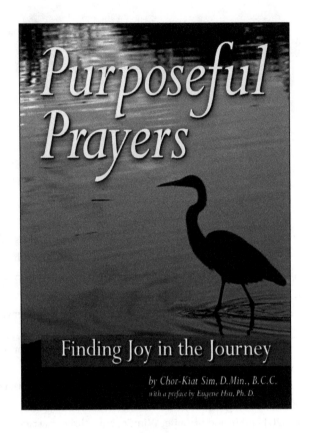

Purposeful Prayers

Prayers

Finding Joy in the Journey

by Chor-Kiat Sim, D.Min., B.C.C.
with a preface by Eugene Hsu, Ph. D.

More from the Author

Readers who wish to enhance their prayer
walk may also enjoy *Purposeful Prayers: Finding Joy
in the Journey* by Dr. Chor-Kiat Sim. Twenty-two
thoughtful, Christ-centered prayers to accompany
you on your spiritual journey and enrich your
prayer experience. Available on Amazon at
http://bit.ly/PurposefulPrayers.

CPSIA information can be obtained
at www.ICGtesting.com
Printed in the USA
FSHW011703130619

9 781545 628249